First published in May 2008

ISBN 978-0-9556564-7-7
ISBN 978-0-9556564-8-4 (de Luxe edition)

Published by
Porter Press International

PO Box 2, Tenbury Wells,
WR15 8XX, UK.
Tel: +44 (0)1584 781588
Fax: +44 (0)1584 781630
sales@porterpress.co.uk
www.porterpress.co.uk

Designed by Grafx Resource
Printed and bound in China through World Print Limited

The Automotive Art Of Alan Fearnley

Design by Andrew Garman

Porter Press International

To my sons, Gavin and Lee, with pride and great affection.

ACKNOWLEDGEMENTS

My thanks go to the following people who have helped see this project through. Firstly, Philip Porter has been the navigator on this small literary rally and got us through all the tricky bits with great skill, organisation and aplomb.

I am exceptionally grateful to Murray Walker for giving up his valuable time to pen the Foreword, and his very kind words.

I greatly appreciate Stirling Moss sharing his memories with us and giving some fascinating glimpses of the stories behind some of my pictures. Who could be more authoritative?

My particular thanks to Andy Garman, of *Grafx Resource*, for his excellent layout and design work. Even his vast experience and expertise with modern technology has been stretched by the challenge of obtaining the standard of reproduction I wanted. Michael Mills of *Colourhouse* has assisted Andy in meeting that challenge.

The backroom team at Porter Press, in Worcestershire, have done a splendid job and my thanks to Leanne Banks and Mary Fulford-Talbot, and especially Abigail Humphries and Claire Bryan. Though based the other side of the World in New Zealand, Mark Holman read through the proofs with his expert eye backed by a great depth of knowledge of motoring history.

Finally, my thanks to my great friends, Alan Stephenson and Eric Jackson, for contributing their thoughts on the paintings they own and which are reproduced in this book.

CONTENTS

FOREWORD

The magic of motorsport with its unique blend of vivid personalities, the interaction of man and machine, its colour, noise, drama, danger and worldwide travel has been one of the driving forces of my life. I am the proud possessor of a large library of books which I have built up over the years to remind me of the great times I have lived through. They are almost entirely illustrated with superb photographs which brilliantly communicate every aspect and detail of the sport I love but on my study walls I have paintings, including a magnificent impression by the iconic Gordon Crosby of my father winning the 1928 Ulster Grand Prix motor cycle race at record speed. It dominates the room with its sheer drama for there is something about outstanding artwork, executed by the hand of man, which invests it with a very special emotional appeal.

It isn't easy though. To get it right the motorsport artist has to have an intuitive feel for his subject, command of composition and perspective, mechanical accuracy, landscape reproduction, figure work and action. In the history of our sport there have been precious few who have been able to rise above the ordinary by combining all these talents and, for me, Alan Fearnley is amongst the very finest of all time. His work stirs my pulse and commands my infinite respect. The pages which follow are a cornucopia of creative riches which, by virtue of the fact that they are literally hand-made impressions of a moment in time rather than mechanical reproductions, have unique appeal. My admiration and respect for Alan's ability to produce such brilliant work is profound.

We first met when BBC TV opened its coverage of the incredible 1988 Monaco Grand Prix with scenes from Alan's one-man show in the Salon Beaumarchais at the Hôtel de Paris and I was immediately impressed with his modesty, charm and sense of humour - a combination of characteristics that I wouldn't necessarily have expected from someone of his artistic status. He found his forte by way of progressing from colouring prints in a photo studio to becoming an impressionist painter and then to landscape and transport subjects but, although he is famous for his magnificent paintings of railway and aviation subjects, cars are his first love and we motor racing enthusiasts are all the luckier because of it. What is more, although it has nothing to do with motor racing, the fact that he is also a nifty saxophone player further endears him to Big Band enthusiast Murray Walker!

As you turn the pages which follow, you will be able to revel in the joy of viewing artistic impressions which are not only painstakingly accurate from the mechanical point of view but which portray the equally important *people* just as accurately and which absolutely ooze drama and excitement. It is all there in evocative detail from that sensational victory of Christian Lautenschlager's Mercedes over George Boillot's Peugeot in the 1914 French Grand Prix to the 2007 Red Bull F1 car, by way of the Silver Arrows and Bugattis of the '30s, Le Mans, the TT, the Mille Miglia, the Grands Prix of the '50s and '60s and, as you will see, so much more.

I am honoured to know Alan Fearnley and privileged to include his work in my collection.

Enjoy!

Murray Walker
Hampshire
January, 2008

Photo: Abigail Humphries

INTRODUCTION

It was about two years ago that Carole and I were having dinner with Philip and Julie Porter while we were all attending the Monaco Historique Meeting for classic competition cars, a wonderful event so different in atmosphere and ethos to the Formula One GP that takes place a few days later. The subject of my first book, *The Classic Car Paintings of Alan Fearnley*, cropped up and Philip casually mentioned that, if I ever thought of doing another one, Porter Press would be very interested in publishing it. Needless to say, with his background in writing books and publishing, his expertise, knowledge, friends and connections, I was immediately enthusiastic about the project. However, these things never happen overnight and so here I am, two years later, writing the Introduction to my second book of motoring paintings.

Sometimes people say to me, often with a rather wistful, starry-eyed expression on their face, that it must be wonderful to be an artist and just spend your whole life doing only what you want to do. And I agree with them because it is, but not, perhaps, quite in the way that they imagine. Painting to commission, sometimes to a deadline, coming up with enough ideas to complete an exhibition by the date the gallery has been booked, etc., are not too dissimilar from other professions. Although I can't pretend the stress levels are quite on a par with those of a brain surgeon or prime minister, it is quite different to spending a few happy hours at the easel on a Sunday afternoon.

However, I can't think of anything that I would rather do, although I think being an author or composer would probably be an equally enjoyable life, with much the same plusses and minuses. For well over 30 years now I have worked when I wanted, which in fact has been most of the time, and had days off whenever there was something I wanted to do or watch. To live like this, doing a job one loves and making a reasonable living into the bargain, is, I think, about as much as one can reasonably ask for in a working life.

For the past 25 years my painting output has been largely based on motoring subjects. When I started, many of my pictures were of the Edwardian races of the early years of the last century, perhaps inspired by the works of Gordon-Crosby. Then came a period up to the late '90s, when my output was very largely based on the modern Formula One scene, the picture often being published as limited edition prints, usually co-signed by the drivers portrayed – stars like Senna, Mansell and Prost. For the past 10 years, however, I have turned more and more to compositions based around period cars, and scenes and events from the classic period between 1930 and 1965. This has coincided with my interest in, and appreciation of, older cars.

In some magazine I have, there is an article on the 1938 V12 Lagonda. The author starts with the sentence, "To sit behind the wheel of this car is to be confronted by an ergonomic nightmare". To me, that sentence seems to sum up what is so good about modern cars and what is so interesting and joyous about older ones. I am fortunate to own a 1951 Jaguar XK 120, still in broadly original condition, but a little moth-eaten around the edges which suits me very well. To feel the same verve and excitement as driving the XK around a country lane at 60, you would have to do double that speed in the latest Aston on Ferrari. And I somehow feel that the grin would be much less broad in the modern car. The other old car in my stable is a 1934 Lagonda M45, the second I have owned. This one was bought as a rolling chassis having lost its original saloon coachwork in the 1960s and I am slowly bringing it back to life with an open two-seater body. As only this will be new and the rest of the car will be from 1934, I am hoping it will still have all those peculiarities, foibles and annoyances that it would have had when originally built.

Besides my work giving me the opportunity to be around and involved with wonderful machinery, perhaps the greatest good fortune has been to meet the people I have. Many of my customers are great characters with wonderful stories to tell and I am proud and pleased to say that many of them are now numbered amongst my closest friends. It has also been my great good fortune to meet many of the stars I saw hurtling past me as I stood on the embankments at Oulton Park and Silverstone in the early '60s. Even more amazing to me is that those stars have included six Formula One World Champions, one of them the man many regard as the greatest, and I think certainly the most legendary, Juan Manuel Fangio. He spent the best part of three days with us whilst signing prints at one of my many Monaco exhibitions. Some of these great men - Roy Salvadori and Stirling Moss for instance - have been particularly generous in giving me their time, reminiscences and recollections.

So that sums up my life as a motoring artist. I've leaned against some of the world's greatest cars, been given rides in one or two of them and met some wonderful people including many of the giants of the motor racing world. Oh – and I've painted some pictures as well. A selection of them appear in this volume and I hope they give an idea of the range and scope of my output and art, and impart some pleasure and perhaps stir a few memories as well.

Alan Fearnley, Ilkley, West Yorkshire

INSPIRATION AND TECHNIQUE

Ideas for painting subjects find their way onto the canvas from many different sources and by many different routes. Occasionally, and I suppose I should say, very occasionally, there is a 'eureka moment' - the proverbial flash of inspiration, and an idea seems to frame itself in the mind as if by magic. This is, though, a very rare occurrence and more usually it will come as the result of a scene actually seen, the depiction of an event that I think should be painted, or the desire to use in a picture a certain type of car that I find particularly attractive.

As can perhaps be seen from the contents of this volume, this last fund of inspiration can lead to a certain repetitiveness in the choice of subject matter. I have done many, many paintings portraying Speed Six Bentleys with drophead coachwork reminiscent of the style of Gurney Nutting, pre-War open Lagondas of all shapes and sizes but usually 45s, Jaguar XK 120s and, of course, just about any Ferrari with a V12 engine at the front. As far as locations are concerned, they are, of course, unlimited. Sometimes country scenes are simply made up or loosely based on a location I know, but often, although the picture is imaginary, I will introduce specific trees or features I know into the scene. I also find myself much drawn to use French villages in my paintings. Often they have an unspoilt, unchanging charm but without the 'chocolate

box' tweeness that I personally associate with the thatched roof prettiness of some English villages. I like to portray what we have done so often ourselves. Parking the old car in the shade of a lime or plane tree in a village square whilst enjoying a coffee and croissant in a nearby café strikes an immediate 'rapprochement' with many an old car enthusiast who has done exactly the same thing.

The other source of subject matter for very many paintings is work commissioned by individual clients. The big difference is, of course, that many of the decisions are not made entirely on my own preferences or on the demands of the painting as I see it. In a commissioned work these are decided by the wishes of the client and what he thinks is important in his picture.

When portraying an actual event, not only are the cars involved a known constituent but also the time of day, season of the year, weather conditions, etc., are established and unchangeable. It is up to me to arrange and combine those elements into a worthwhile pictorial composition. With other subjects, perhaps more personal to the client with, for instance, the car outside their home or at their favourite picnic spot, we have to work together to achieve not only the painting they want, but also one that I wish to paint. Usually we are able to manage that but not always and, occasionally, I end up declining the work and the client has to find another artist more in tune with his views.

The actual process of painting follows much the same pattern with every picture. I have used the same basic palette of colours for over 40 years and, for the interest of those readers who also paint, they are Raw and Burnt Sienna, Burnt Umber, Cadmium Red Hue, Alizarin Crimson, Cadmium Yellow Hue, Cerulean and Ultramarine Blue and Titanium White. I might also occasionally add Chrome Lemon and Viridian Green to these.

I start by covering the white of the canvas with a thin brownish wash and drawing out the composition on that. Often the more critical parts of the painting - the cars or the people - will have been drawn out a dozen times already on a layout pad until I am satisfied with the angle or stance of that particular feature. However, when transforming it to the canvas I only need the outline correct as I will use the drawing as a reference and put all the detail in in the paint.

I then concentrate on getting the general tonal areas of the canvas covered with the main elements plainly indicated to try and establish the overall 'feel' of the picture. The main features are then worked up in more detail toward their correct colour values before once again moving to work on the background areas. At this time it may become apparent that some adjustments need to be made, perhaps some element to be moved higher or lower in the composition or the need for some addition or subtraction to the balance of it.

In this way, the picture progresses with the final stages usually being the most intricate

areas of detail. These I often try to abbreviate with a highlight or flick of brushwork that, if successful, looks far more convincing than slavishly setting out each spoke or rivet head. It then only remains to frame and exhibit, or present to the client with fingers crossed, hoping that we did both had the same idea in mind when we shook hands all those weeks previously.

'Trees At Sunset' 1966. This is an example of the sort of painting I used to do during my Impressionist landscape days in the sixties. As you can see, I was clearly influenced by a certain Claude Monet.

See the completed painting on page 115

ALPINE DESCENT

One of the most famous of all Jaguars, NUB 120, was the XK 120 campaigned with tremendous success by Ian Appleyard and his wife Pat, who navigated and was actually the daughter of Sir William Lyons, the founder of Jaguar Cars.

Appleyard did particularly well in the Alpine Rally, winning a coveted Coupe de Alpes for a penalty-free run in 1950 and 1951. When he and NUB 120 repeated the feat in 1952, he won the first ever Gold Cup to be awarded for three successive Coupes. Here they are charging down a typical gritty mountain road.

In fact, Appleyard had first won a Coupe with his SS Jaguar 100 in 1948 and took a fifth such award in 1953 with his second XK 120, which was registered RUB 120.

APPLEYARD'S FIRST ALPINE

Collection: Mr. P. Gallegos (16" x 12")

Collection: Mr. A. Billett (16" x 12")

SILVER AND RED

I think that I managed to get as much movement into this picture as I have into any racing painting I've ever done. It shows eventual winner Nuvolari in the D-type Auto Union leading Von Brauchitsch in the Mercedes W154 through Red Gate corner at the Donington Grand Prix of 1938.

The sketchy nature of the brushwork and the slightly drifting attitude of the cars, along with the dust being kicked up from the inside of the track by the Mercedes, all combine to give the sense of action and speed.

Collection: Mr. M. Drayton (16" x 12")

Collection: Mr. D. Tansy (16" x 12")

Lucky Number

Having done a little bit of amateur racing and run cars and karts with my son, I feel a great affinity with the amateur team, teams that build and prepare their own cars in house, garage and garden shed surrounded by oil cans, tool boxes, axle stands, etc., which are always in the way or being tripped over.

I tried to capture that atmosphere in this picture of a young driver painting his racing number on his Aston Martin ready for the next day's race watched over by his, undoubtedly unpaid, 'team'.

Collection: Mr. J. Mason (48" x 24")

COTTON CLUB

I thought I would put these two paintings in as a little light relief and something completely different to my car paintings. I've been a jazz fan all my life and my music preferences coincide with my preferences in cars. i.e. 1930 to the mid 1960s. I had done a few oil sketches of jazz musicians for my friend and publisher, John Mason, when he asked me to do a large painting of a club scene from the roaring twenties. The venue is intended to be somewhere like the Cotton Club and I was able to give myself full rein with the characters and expressions.

CONCERT IN ST MARKS

The St. Marks Square scene came about after we had holidayed in Venice and had spent an evening in the square drinking very expensive wine and coffee and listening to two small orchestras competing with each other at opposite sides. In spite of the commercialism, the atmosphere was wonderful and I resolved to paint the scene for myself but with a rather more elegantly dressed crowd.

Collection Of The Artist (36" x 24")

PRIDE AND PREJUDICE

Some years ago I did a painting, reproduced in the first book of my classic car paintings, of a Rolls-Royce Phantom, parked in a similar street to this, being evaluated by a couple of passing tramps whilst their dog was obviously thinking of relieving itself against one of the car's wheels. An American client was very taken with the picture, and the humour in it, and asked if I could do something similar but using his Lagonda LG6 Rapide Tourer - a car which I believe is unique.

After a great deal of thought and several false starts, this is what I came up with. I tried to give the new owner and his wife suitably superior expressions and their long-suffering neighbours equally appropriate bored ones! The street sweeper's dog, perhaps an Alvis fan, is thinking of passing judgement against the rear wheel.

PICNIC AT THE SHOW

Collection: Mr. D. Stone-Lee (24" x 16")

Collection: Mr. R. Roy (40" x 22")

CLASH OF TITANS

I have painted the 1937 Monaco Grand Prix many times. Not only was it the year that saw one of motor racing's greatest battles but the race featured the Mercedes W125s. Besides being one of the greatest of all Grand Prix cars, the W125 was, to my eyes, also one of the most beautiful. I have done paintings of them coming up the hill at Beau Rivage, through the Casino Square and two or three times around the Station Hairpin.

Here the two protagonists, Von Brauchitsch, No. 10, and Caracciola, have left the Gasworks Hairpin and are thundering along behind the pits in front of the grandstands and royal box. As many people know, Von Brauchitsch went on to win, disobeying team orders.

"Would I have liked to have raced in that period? No. I say no, but that was because I enjoyed my period so much. I might well have enjoyed this as much as my era. I certainly would have enjoyed it far more than the modern era. It was a very passionate sport then. Power is a lot of fun. The more power you've got, the more it requires your attention. Greater concentration is needed." **Sir Stirling Moss**

Collection: Mr. A. Brownridge (24" x 14")

NICE CAR, MONSIEUR

This Jaguar belongs to my pal John Shute and is parked 'somewhere in France'. I think this picture works rather well for a painting of a modern car. I say that because most modern cars tend to be visually rather bland compared with their '50s and '60s counterparts.

However, in this case, the XK8 is a very good-looking car and the colour in it blends very nicely with the warm tones of the stone walls and the road. And rural France is so unchanging that a car like this can be put in such a setting and look entirely at home. The lady in pink only just bears a resemblance to his wife Dianne but, more by luck than judgement, the chap in the white shirt is a pretty good likeness of Shuty.

Collection: Mr. J. Shute (30" x 20")

Collection: Mr. G. Neave (24" x 18")

LAST CUSTOMER

It is possible, as an artist, to bring beauty to a scene that, if one were there, would actually be pretty miserable. Here we have a gentleman who has stopped to fill up his drophead Lagonda LG6 at the village garage on a wet, dark and wintry evening in the early post-war years.

The charm of the picture is in the subtle, almost monotone, warm greeny-greys and the sparkle of the lights and reflections.

LAST TRAIN

Collection Of The Artist (20" x 20")

ASTON PRIVATEER

A nice little oil sketch of the Morris-Goodall/Hitchen Aston Martin Ulster at Le Mans in 1937 with a conversation group around the back of it. It is often an awkward decision knowing just when to stop work on this kind of picture and say, "That's it – it's finished". Should the car and figure on the right have been a little more finished? I shall never know – it might have looked better or possibly not as good, but that decision was made and I'm very happy with it as it is.

It is interesting to compare this with the other painting in this book of Donkin's Ulster at Le Mans in 1935. Both cars were No. 31, and both finished eleventh in the race, but Donkin's car was faster in a very wet year at 69.5mph against the 67.6mph of the Morris-Goodall car in a dry year.

THE BRIDGE AT CHELSWORTH

Collection: Mr. J. Young (22" x 18")

Collection: Mr. M. Woodnutt (10" x 8")

CARRIAGES AT ONE

An entirely made-up picture but one which I felt worked extremely well and really liked to the extent that we had it printed as our Christmas card one year.

I think the exuberance and vitality of the moment comes across really well as these gay young things leave a party in the late twenties, climbing into their supercars of the period. This has been brought about, not only by the drawing and expressions of the figures, but also by the context of the deep shadow and sparkle on the cars.

"The painting of the evening scene is a really nostalgic piece, encompassing elegant cars and beautiful people enjoying a lovely evening in a wonderful setting - maybe tapping into a yearning for times gone by. My wife bought the painting to celebrate our 30th wedding anniversary, and Alan created a special number plate on one of the cars, just for us. It attracts and creates lots of interest - a real conversation piece." **Alan Stephenson**

Collection: Mr. A. Stephenson (40" x 24")

ULSTER THROUGH THE ESSES

This is the Aston Martin Ulster of P. L. Donkin and Lord Hamilton coming through the Esses at Le Mans in 1935 followed by the eventual winner, the Lagonda number four. The Esses at Le Mans is a location painted many times by every artist who tackles motoring subjects and I think we all use the silhouetted photographers at the apex of the first bend as a dramatic motif. I'm not sure I ever get the contours of the road quite right but I think this example worked particularly well with the freedom and looseness of the brushwork.

The client lives in Northern Ireland and I was a little surprised when he said he would collect the painting until he turned up in a lovely old Talbot coupé that he had just collected and was taking back home

In the race, the car finished 11th at an average speed of 69.5mph.

Collection: Mr. J. Kealty (20" x 16")

SUNSHINE AND SHADOW

In 1992, I did a painting of an XK 120 beside a river with a man leaning against the car, and an attractive lady dipping her foot in the water. It was published in several magazines and produced as a limited edition print which sold out very quickly. Since then, I have had many requests for commissions to paint cars and couples beside rivers. This is a nice example of the genre with, I think, a pleasing subtlety of colours in spite of the vivid red E-type.

A key to putting people predominantly in a painting is to have them, wherever possible, wearing large hats that render them unrecognisable. Otherwise it looks likes a couple of strangers set with the client's car.

SUMMER OF '61

Collection: Mr. A. Billett (30" x 20")

Collection: Mrs. J. Coppin (24" x 16")

DAPPLED IN GALLO FLY

The Ferrari Dino, belonging to my friend Alan Stephenson, is seen parked in front of his home. Yellow is probably my least favourite colour for a car in reality, but in paint it looks good and particularly in a sun-dappled scene such as this. It turned out to be, perhaps, my favourite painting of several I have done for Alan.

"The Dino painting is very special to me. As a Ferrari enthusiast, the lines of the Dino are breathtaking. Alan's artistic eye, setting the car at the entrance to our home, with its dappled light, is magnificent. The car is wonderful, but the painting is better." **Alan Stephenson**

Collection: Mr. A. Stephenson (16" x 12")

LOW FLYING MISSILE

When Michael Drayton commissioned me to do a painting of Moss in the Mille Miglia, he sent me a copy of Denis Jenkinson's report of the race printed in Motor Sport, with several sections that he thought would make a good subject underlined. However, the incident shown was his first choice.

Jenks reported that when they drove the course while practising in a 300 SL, they noticed the bump in the long straight section of the road south of Ancona, but at 80mph it didn't register as a problem. When they hit it in the race in the 300 SLR, they were doing nearer 180mph and they simply took off! He tells how suddenly the thunderous drumming of the tyres and suspension ceased and he and Moss glanced at each other in silence for a few seconds as they flew through the air. Fortunately, Moss held the wheel dead straight and, after what must have been a considerable distance, landed and hurtled on to eventual victory.

The low viewpoint was necessary to show the car off the ground and white road line to show the hump in the road.

"We came down this road which was dead straight. Jenks had given me the 'flat-out' signal and we just didn't realise there was this hump in the road. We took off and everything went soft. I thought, 'My God, I mustn't move my hands here'. It just landed. There was really no drama. The only drama was in our minds. We looked at each other and gestured, and knew we'd done wrong! At least we didn't lose any time." **Sir Stirling Moss**

Collection: Mr. M. Drayton (16" x 12")

Collection: Mr. I. Maxwell-Scott (20" x 16")

ASTONS AT THE HOTEL DE FRANCE

We have stayed a couple of times at the Hôtel de France in La Chartre sur Loire that was used in the 1950s as Aston Martin's base when competing at the Le Mans 24-hour race. The impression one gets is that it has not changed, though most of the foliage seen in this picture, in the alley leading to the hotel garage, has now gone.

The inspiration for the picture came from a photograph I came across which was actually a view from the other direction, from the square into the alley with the cars glimpsed through a small crowd of men and boys watching the goings on in the Aston camp.

I changed it round to get a better view of the cars, the action and the view out into the square. DBR 1 number 3 was the car driven by Brooks and Trintignant in 1958. Number two was Moss's and that is intended to be him, with his back to us, talking to John Wyer, the redoubtable Team Manager.

THOROUGHBREDS ALL

LE CONSULAT

Collection: Mr. M. Lovatt (22" x 18")

I was particularly pleased with the title I came up with for this painting with its, hopefully obvious, reference to the cars, the horses and the elegant lady riding side-saddle. This was one of our favourite paintings when I hung it in my one-man London show in 2003 and we were surprised when only one person made a move to buy it.

His wife's friend, however, was heard to say, "You can't buy that, for heaven's sake. It's hunting," and the sale fell through. Quite why a painting of huntsmen and cars can be seen as being supportive of hunting is quite beyond me, but Carole and I are quite pleased as, in spite of a few offers since, the picture still hangs over our fireplace!

Collection Of The Artist (36" x 24")

WILLIAMS IN THE MONACO PITS '29

When I was exhibiting in Monaco in the 1990s, I met a croupier from the casino who told me he'd seen every Monaco G.P., watching the first as a boy of nine in the late twenties.

The Monaco pits have changed a great deal since those days but the bridge, and some of the buildings in the background, were still there hiding among the new high-rise blocks of apartments.

It appears from period photographs that drivers, mechanics and friends seemed to spend a lot of time lounging around the cars on practice and race days which gives an artist free reign to come up with a scene like this, with eventual winner William Grover Williams sitting on the wheel of his Bugatti chatting to friends in front of the similar car of the Swiss driver Lepori. Beyond them, Rigal goes out to practice in Alfa number 24.

Collection: Mr. M. de Ferranti (24" x 28")

DUNDROD HAIRPIN

Awet day can add a great deal to paintings of this type of subject. The spray from the wheels and glints of reflections in the road give movement and vitality to the action. The scene is the 1955 T.T. at Dundrod, a tragic race that claimed the lives of three of the drivers.

Moss, the rear of his Mercedes wrecked by a blown tyre, is about to pass Hawthorn in the Jaguar and go on to win the race in what was, perhaps, his greatest year, a season during which he also won the Mille Miglia and the Targa Florio.

"The tread blew off at Dundrod during the Tourist Trophy, I didn't hit anything. In this painting, I am coming up to pass Mike Hawthorn. It was pouring with rain and I liked the rain. I suppose that was one of my best victories. I had to make up quite a bit of time after my enforced pit stop but I enjoyed that situation, having a go." **Sir Stirling Moss**

"I am very proud to own a painting by Alan, whom I, like many others, consider to be one of the very finest motoring artists in the World. His ability to capture the atmosphere of a scene, accurately represent the cars and portray appropriate figures is brilliant. Indeed, I think it is his 'people' that really bring life to his paintings, making them absolutely exceptional. In this painting, the two photographers underline my point – adding period detail and a sense of drama.

"As to the cars, the Jaguar D-type is, for me, the classic post-war sports car, a veritable aircraft on wheels that saw the brilliant aerodynamicist, Malcolm Sayer, use a longhand version of computer-aided design to create pure art. The Mercedes-Benz 300SLR was a very worthy rival that, due to the sheer genius of Stirling Moss, won three of the great sports car classics in 1955. In the TT he had a fine battle with the Jaguar team leader, the charismatic, Mike Hawthorn.

"I have written several books with Stirling, my boyhood hero, and the first was on his truly amazing 1955 season. This wonderful painting brings it all alive and encapsulates this fabulous period." **Philip Porter**

Collection: Mr. P.H. Porter (24" x 16")

Private Collection (20" x 16")

Just Needs A Little Work

This type of subject is not everyone's cup of tea but I enjoy painting them, creating the whimsical amusement and introducing all the detail and odds and ends of detritus necessary for the scene.

The situation is obvious and features in the daydreams of many an enthusiast – finding a decrepit old M45 Lagonda rusting in a barn and ripe for restoration.

The farmer looks fairly resolute and the farmhand and dog wait for the haggling to begin.

SPECIAL STAGE

This is Californian Peter Read taking part in the 2002 Scottish Malts Rally. The Aston he is driving is a very special car, being the 1955 Monte Carlo Rally class winner driven by Gatsonides.

I drove up to Blair Athol to see them leave the start line on this special stage. Unfortunately, by this time the team had had so many mishaps they were no longer in a reasonable points scoring position. So, after the stage, we all, including the guy in the picture with the motor bike (a friend of Peter's doing the Rally with them), went down to the local hostelry to pass an hour before they set off to catch up with the rally and head back to England.

Collection: Mr. P. Read (36" x 24")

THE SQUARE, FLAYOSC

This painting shows Simon Moore's beautiful Alfa Romeo parked near his holiday home in France. The car is one of the rarest of the rare, a 1935 8c 2900 A, and probably the one that finished third in the 1936 Mille Miglia.

The car's history is quite amazing and too long for me to do it justice. In brief, it came to England just before the Second World War and during the War passed to Tony Crook of Bristol Cars fame. When hostilities ceased, the car went to America where the engine was plucked as a spare for an Indianapolis car, the chassis was used in a plastic-bodied special and the body utilised in a Ford-engined hot rod.

Amazingly, all the components survived and, in 1980, Simon took on the Herculean task of bringing them all together again over the next four years and then restoring them over another four years. That he managed to accomplish this justifies, I think, some sort of medal from the classic car world. Certainly the opportunity to come into contact with, and paint, a wonderful machine like this makes me realise just how lucky I am in my chosen profession.

Collection: Mr. S. Moore (30" x 20")

53

SUNDAY MORNING CHORES

Carole and I went to stay with Roger and Christine Newman so that I could get the reference for this painting of Roger's Jaguars. The original parts of the house are very old and, as we were being shown around, Roger pointed out some of the original exposed beams and recalled that the house was already 200 years old when Henry VIII came to the throne.

It made a very pleasing and natural setting for a fine collection of Jaguars. The little dog was no longer with us at the time of the commission but must have been fondly remembered as the Newmans were keen that it should be portrayed with the cars.

Collection: Mr. & Mrs. R. Newman (30" x 24")

55

Collection: Mr. I. Maxwell-Scott (36" x 20")

A CERTAIN STYLE

A great deal of time was spent working out the composition of this picture in order to tell the story as well as create an attractive and dramatic scene. In the end it turned out to be the fastest selling painting I've ever done.

The gentleman concerned was in the North of England on business and, being interested in having a painting done of his Aston Martin, telephoned to see if he could call in for a chat. When he arrived, I had literally taken this picture off the easel minutes earlier and propped it against the studio wall and decided it was finished.

Ian walked in, took one look at it and said, "How much is that?" Within a couple of minutes, the deal was done. The paint had not even started to dry!

Collection: Mr. G. Neave (24" x 20")

THAT'S AT A PLACE CALLED BROOKLANDS

I freely admit that this is a very sentimentalised picture, but I make no apologies. I love Victorian paintings of the waiting fisherman's wife gazing over a stormy sea or a wronged young lady with blank expression and some cad's letter in her hand. I see this image as being an extension of that school of painting.

The old man, walking stick, dog and just-glimpsed leather crash helmet in the opened suitcase in front of the dusty old Aston all strike a contrast of age with the grandson in his sweatshirt, jeans and trainers.

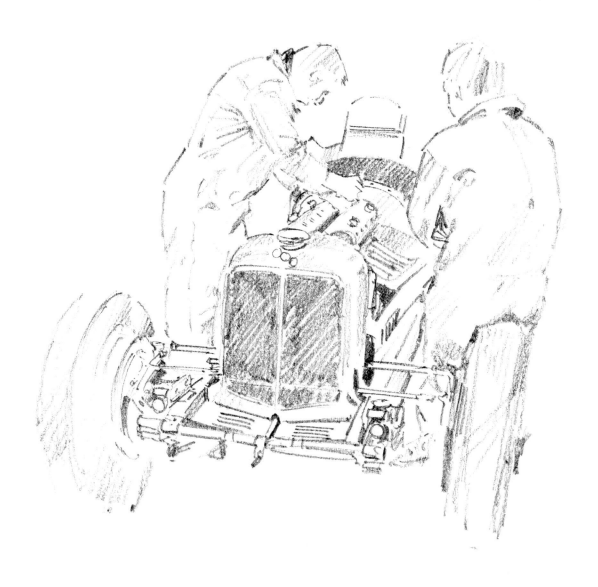

JAGUAR'S DAY DAWNING

Paintings are not always easy to title and it has to be admitted that often titles are contrived, silly or sometimes pompous. However, in this particular case, I thought the title spot on. The C-type Jaguar of Whitehead and Walker, with dawn breaking behind it, is on its way to winning the 1951 Le Mans 24 Hour race.

This was the C-type's first race, first time out and the first of Jaguar's successes at Le Mans that were to establish the marque's reputation. It is a wonderfully romantic story and one which I attempted to capture in the drama and atmosphere of this painting.

Jaguar Engineering Director, Bill Heynes, convinced Bill Lyons that the one surviving C-type, though it had a lead of three-quarters of an hour, needed to speed up and the Jaguar Chairman communicated this to his Team Manager, 'Lofty' England.

"Bloody hell! I didn't want us to lose the whole lot, so I put out a signal that didn't look any different from 'OK'. 'Don't think they can see that signal, England,' said the Old Man, so then I did as I was told. On the next lap, of course, Walker's time was about 20 seconds quicker. 'That's too fast, he'll break it,' said the Old Man. So I put out a 'Go Slow' signal. 'That's too slow now'.

"I'd had enough of this. Peter Whitehead was about to take over, so I gave him a stopwatch and told him to time himself going past the Hippodrome on the straight, and to ignore all my signals unless they said, 'stop' or 'go like bloody hell'. And that's what he did. 'They aren't paying any attention to your signals, England.' 'Aren't they, Mr. Lyons? Very difficult to see you know.'" **'Lofty' England**

Collection: Mr. P. Jervell (32" x 20")

A CORNER IN PIGALLE

This is a little painting based on a photograph that I snapped in Paris, but I don't think it was actually in Pigalle - it just seemed an appropriate location!

Without having any particularly outstanding points, the picture is one of my favourites. The rather impressionistic handling of the light and shade and the people sitting outside the café, the silhouetted figure against the farther background and the Alfa with two wheels propped on the pavement, all combine to make it, for me, a very satisfying whole.

THOROUGHBRED STABLE

Private Collection   (30" x 20")

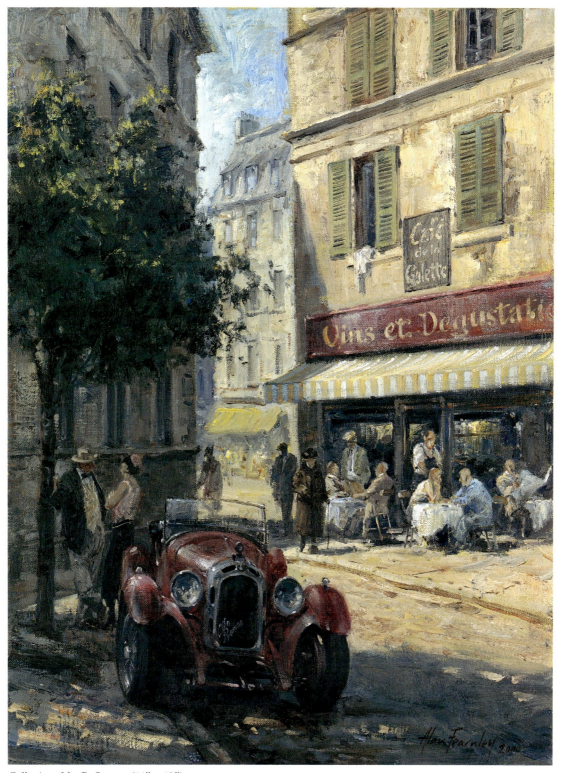

Collection: Mr. B. Suggett (16" x 12")

READY TO GO

An oil sketch of Nuvolari anxiously waiting for his mechanic to finish hammering the rear wheel spinners on his 8CM Maserati somewhere in 1933.

The picture works particularly well because of the loose, first time brush work and the deep shadows that give a feeling of vitality and action to the scene.

Collection: Mr. B. Suggett (8" x 7")

Collection: Mercedes-Benz UK (36" x 24")

ULTIMATE TRUCKING

This picture was commissioned by Mercedes Benz UK on the occasion of their winning the European Truck Racing Championship. The spectacle of these huge machines wheel to wheel at speeds of over 100mph was quite amazing and in the wet, as here at Brands Hatch, even more so.

The painting was unveiled at a Mercedes corporate event where I met the racing driver, and ex-motor cycle champion, Steve Parrish. He'd parked his 500SL in the car park with its personal number plate PEN15, which I thought gave an indication of the sort of bravado you'd expect from a truck racing champion!

MONACO NIGHT

This is a slightly different treatment of a Monaco night scene in Casino Square. Less detailed with the subjects dissolving into the lights of the casino and without the glitzy dresses and wraps that I use in the larger compositions, it, nevertheless, conveys, I hope, the atmosphere of opulence and glamour one would expect of this location.

"I have always admired Alan Fearnley's paintings.

"He is one of the greatest true artists who can portray real nostalgic scenes of old motor sport events so realistically that you can almost smell the Castrol R. But in addition, his ability to depict old classic cars in romantic situations is outstanding and sets him apart from any other artist.

"So, having competed in a number of Monte Carlo Rallies myself, as soon as I saw this red SS100 in its 1930s' atmospheric setting outside the famous Casino in Casino Square, I fell for it like a ton of bricks. 'The Lady in Red; she had to be mine'!"
Eric Jackson

Collection: Mr. E. Jackson (16" x 12")

OUT FOR A BLOW

For me, this painting has a real sense of space and openness and the feeling of the wind blowing through it. The view, which looks as though it could be anywhere, is actually looking up the Wharfe Valley towards where I live from the hill called Otley Chevin, though the lovely ragged Scots Pine tree actually stands outside a friend's house at Beamsley a few miles further up the valley.

The car is a T7-bodied Lagonda M45 of about 1935 and the dogs started off as fox hounds but somehow ended up looking rather like Weimaraners.

Collection: Mr. A. Billett (30" x 24")

Collection: Mr. R. Gathercole (40" x 30")

Ferrari's F1 Drivers (Pre-1991)

To be honest, I can't remember exactly why I painted this picture. It was published as a poster but I'm not sure that was the reason for doing the painting. However, it was exhibited that year, 1991, at the Essen Motor Show in Germany where, on the exhibition stand, I had agreed to actually paint a picture whilst my co-exhibitor, the American sculptor, Paul Nesse, worked on a clay model.

I think we both hated the experience in equal measure! However, one of the good things that transpired was that I was invited to a luncheon thronged with legendary racing drivers. Luigi Villoresi made a speech (in Italian) and I have a photograph which shows Phil Hill, Innes Ireland, Roy Salvadori, Olivier Gendebien, Chris Amon and Cliff Allison sitting round having coffee afterwards. It still amazes me to think I was actually there.

OVERTIME

Anyone who has done any amateur motor sport will know that this nice, intimate little picture portrays part of the job description - working into the early hours of the morning in order to get the car ready for the next day's race.

The car in the foreground is, of course, a Brooklands Riley. The Alta on its axle stands behind is the car owned and raced by Martin Redmond, who happens to be one of my closest friend's next door neighbours.

The dog, needless to say, won't go home until everyone else does.

Collection: Mr. H. Bell (16" x 12")

MOUNTAIN TRIALLING

This painting is of an imaginary scene during the 1913 Alpine Trial and shows the Rolls-Royce Silver Ghost of James Radley. These cars are sometimes known, though apparently not amongst Rolls-Royce aficionados, as the Alpine Eagle but are, I believe, more correctly called the 'Continental' Silver Ghost.

In 1912, Radley had entered his car for the Alpine Trial and been embarrassed by having to unload two passengers in order to make it to the top of one of the passes. Henry Royce took this failure very seriously and during the following year much testing and development work was done.

In 1913, four cars were entered, including Radley's, and ran faultlessly, completely dominating the event.

Collection Of The Artist (36" x 24")

THE PADDOCK AT ANGOULEME

We first went to the annual race meeting at Angoulême in 2002 after several years of people telling me what a great event it was. The journey was made as part of a classic car tour and we went in my 1935 Lagonda M45.

The Angoulême event is held in the old town part of the city which stands on a hilltop surrounded by the modern urban sprawl and the cars congregate in what looks like a very large boules court, which holds the paddock, and then race on the roads that run up and down the ramparts of the old town. The atmosphere is incredibly laid back and casual and about as far away from a Silverstone Grand Prix as it is possible to imagine. Needless to say, I was completely enchanted. I did this little painting of typical cars parked in the sun-dappled paddock on our return.

Collection: Mr. P. Jervell (16" x 12")

MAESTRO'S MISTAKE

This is another Mille Miglia painting of Moss based on the account written by Denis Jenkinson in Motor Sport magazine. In the early stages of the race, entering the town of Padova, the pair were being harried by Castelotti in the Ferrari who had left one minute after them. Moss braked a fraction late from their 150mph approach to the town centre and bounced off the straw bales at the corner, allowing the Italian through.

I have attempted to tell the story and capture the excitement and action of the moment in the bodies of the drivers and the swirling strands of straw.

"I remember Castellotti coming past for two reasons. Firstly, because he was the only car that passed us. Secondly, he was going unrealistically fast for that early in the race. When he put his foot down, he'd leave a couple of black lines up the road. I remember thinking, 'Boy, he's going to have to change his tyres'. I don't know what his schedule was but I would have thought he'd arranged to have two stops. [Castellotti changed tyres at Ravenna after less than 20% of the race] We did one, although we did throw a few gallons in, it's true, at Pescara but it was really a one-stop race. I would have thought he was reckoning on two because he would never have kept the tyres on and I remember thinking it was probably not that reliable. It was a 4.4-litre straight six, not a V12.

"He was at ten-tenths plus, whereas I was at nine-tenths. I remember following him and it was a very fast car. He had one-and-a-half litres more than us. I remember trying to catch him to encourage him to go even faster and risk the car. He would have won if he'd kept going at that speed but you just couldn't do it. I was keeping to a speed that was as fast as I wanted to go. He probably knew the course better than I did because he'd probably been to Rome a thousand times."
Sir Stirling Moss

Private Collection (16" x 12")

Collection: Mr. P. Read (48" x 30")

NEW KID ON THE BLOCK

A rather fanciful idea this! The new Aston Martin DBR1 stands gleaming and sparkling under the strip lighting in the racing shop at Feltham, whilst two of the outdated DB3Ss are left in the foreground shadows. David Brown leans on the car's headrest behind Roy Salvadori who has his hands in his pockets. At the other side of the car, John Wyer, standing between Stirling Moss and Reg Parnell, makes a point.

The whole thing is a flight of fancy but I thought a novel way of getting a comparison of the two types of Aston Martin sports racer along with some of the key figures of the Aston teams of the 1950s. The painting was made into a successful limited edition print.

"The DB3S - very nice to drive, very nice balance but it would lift its inside wheel and spin. Both the DB3S and DBR1 had 'bastard' gearboxes."
Sir Stirling Moss

CLARK THROUGH

This is the German Grand Prix of 1965 with eventual winner Jim Clark, at the height of his powers in the Lotus, leading second place man, Graham Hill in the BRM and Dan Gurney in third place in the Brabham.

This painting demonstrates very well, I think, the advantages of the painted scene over a photograph. Apart from the fact that, obviously, no photographer could stand where I have placed myself as the artist, photographs of cars swooping through the twists and turns of the Nűrburgring, or any other racing circuit, almost invariably appear static. The instant the shutter is pressed everything - wheels, verges, roadway, etc. - comes to a halt.

With acceptable artistic licence applied to these factors, I don't believe anyone would say that the cars in this picture appear to be doing less than 100mph.

CLARK (LOTUS) HILL (BRM) GURNEY (BRABHAM)   GERMAN G.P. 1965

Collection: Mr. J. Shaw (30" x 20")

C-Type Pit Stop

A small, dashed-off oil sketch of the C-type Jaguar pitting on its way to victory in 1953. The drivers on this occasion were Tony Rolt and Duncan Hamilton, the latter seen climbing out of the car here and recognisable by his red helmet.

I find the C-, D- and E-type Jaguars difficult cars to paint and draw because of the very subtle changes of shape in the bonnet and wings. The free brushwork here contributes to the action of the picture and, I think, I remembered to paint a number onto the Austin Healey before it went off to the customers who bought it – I certainly hope so!

"At about 03.00 hours I went over to the pits. It was just before first light. Wisps of mist on the circuit, and headlights still on. Duncan Hamilton and Tony Rolt were thundering their way to what was to be an historic victory but these, of all times, were to be the critical hours. I went to the entrance to the Jaguar pit and stopped. I saw Angela Hamilton and Lois Rolt, 'Lofty' on the pit counter, various others of the team around the pit. It was silent – the tension was palpable. 'Oh hello, Raymond,' said Angela brightly. 'Would you like a cup of tea?'

"To this day, I find the recollection deeply moving. It epitomised for me what we then all knew it was all about. Curiously like the war. Stiff upper lip. Do what one has to do. Make a joke. Don't make a fuss. Get on with it – and by all means have a helluva party afterwards." **Raymond Baxter**

Into The Sunlight

Collection: Mr. B. Hazell (30" x 20")

Collection: Mr. P. Jervell (10" x 8")

CLARK AT EAU ROUGE

Eau Rouge is, I am informed by people who have driven through it, one of the greatest corners in motor sport but I can tell them, it is also one of the most difficult of which to make a successful painting. I find the actual corner itself, where the cars zig-zag over the bridge, quite impossible, as behind the cars the picture is bound to be filled with nothing but roadway climbing behind them.

So here we are, a hundred yards past the apex, with the usual suspects, Clark, Hill and Gurney in the Lotus, BRM and Brabham, respectively, leading the rest of the field away from the start. In fact, Clark had started from the third row of the grid but was in the lead by the time they came out of the first corner and stayed in front to the chequered flag.

I believe this was the last time that the Lotus team cars ran without the yellow stripe that became their recognised team livery.

Collection: Dr. S. Goodwin (24" x 16")

Collection: Mr. T. Spafford (16" x 12")

THE FOUNTAIN, GORDES

Carole and I have stayed several times in Gordes, a beautiful hilltop village in the Luberon region of France, and I have painted several pictures of different cars parked by the fountain in the square behind the old church. This is artistic licence at its most blatant because I don't believe cars are, in fact, allowed to park there!

However, it is a lovely location to site a nice car with several typical plane trees and the particularly attractive fountain giving the opportunity for several slightly differing views and compositions. In this instance, the fountain provides a backdrop for the only time I've been commissioned to paint a Triumph TR3A.

BREAK FOR A CHAT

I think there is a particularly nice, timeless quality about this picture of Hugh Boucher's lovely old 3-litre Bentley parked in front of his beautiful home in the Kent countryside. The scene is, in fact, just as it appears today and, no doubt, apart from the car, just as it has appeared for several hundred years. Perhaps, because of this, a more modern vehicle would have jarred the senses in much the same way as the old gardener could have had he been holding a strimmer instead of a scythe.

Collection: Mr. H. Boucher (20" x 16")

THE FLOWER SELLER

This has the feeling of a busy little picture with lots going on but, in fact, only the Bugatti, its driver and the flower seller have any amount of detail in them at all. Everything else is just loosely suggested or indicated but make for a colourful, lively and attractive painting.

Collection: Mr. H. Bell (16" x 12")

Collection: Mr. P. Jervell (26" x 14")

FERRARI PITS MONACO '56

The Monaco pits and start area in the pre-modern race era are scenes I have used many times. With the pit counters set up under the trees that divided the two roads that ran to and from the old Gasworks Hairpin, it provides the ideal setting for my love of combining cars with people, portraying styles of dress, imagined get-togethers and occasional portraits.

I hope the pale blue racing suit clad figure leaning against the Dunlop sign is an approximate likeness of Peter Collins - his Ferrari No. 26 is being manoeuvred into place.

Collection: Mr. B. Hazell (30" x 20")

THE COLONEL'S FERRARI

Colonel Ronnie Hoare was the owner of Maranello Concessionaires, the British Ferrari importers and a regular entrant of cars at prestigious race meetings such as Le Mans and the Goodwood Nine Hours. His Ferraris ran with the distinctive blue nose and stripe, plus a Union Jack. This picture is of the Piers Courage and Roy Pike GTB on its way to winning the G.T. category at Le Mans in 1966.

Night scenes are a godsend to the artist when striving for a feeling of drama and tension in a picture and here I have used the forward leaning silhouetted figures and momentous highlights to suggest other figures to bring about these sensations.

Maranello Concessionaires 250 LM. Crow ft '68.

WHAT AN ENTRANCE

We probably all know people like this - the type who arrives late for the party and then arrives in such a way that everyone knows they are there. The situation does, however, give me, as an artist, plenty of scope for figure drawing and expressions and general amusement.

The painting was intended to be in a similar vein to "A Certain Style" pictured elsewhere in this book, but here we have the dashing rogue with his flying helmet and goggles complementing his evening suit, having arrived in his blower Bentley, already casting an eye over the ladies on the veranda as he hands his gauntlets to the footman.

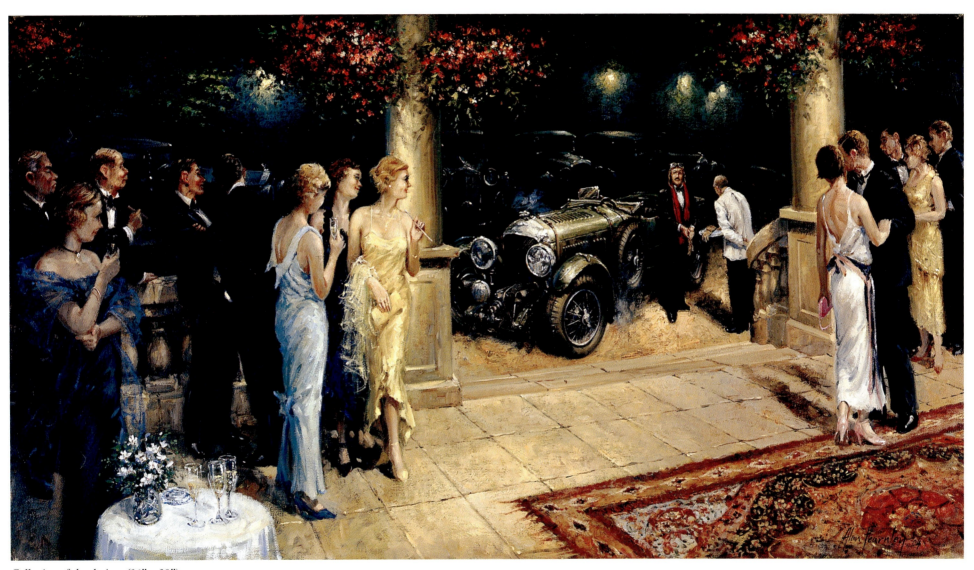

Collection of the Artist   (36" x 20")

BELLA VISTA

The background seen in this painting exists somewhere in, I think, Tuscany and was based on a magazine photograph but I could never discover the location.

The foreground, the soft-coloured stone-paved patio with its ornate lamps and balustrade, is entirely my own creation, conceived to provide a setting for the romantic young couple and their Ferrari SWB California Spyder. The picture title is definitely intended to apply to both the view and the car.

Collection: Mr. B. Suggett (24" x 16")

MONACO '56

Stirling Moss, at his masterful best, led this race from flag to flag. I have pictured the cars streaming away from the start in front of the beautiful old Monégasque townscape, much of which was soon to disappear and be replaced with modern multi-storey blocks of apartments.

In 1956, however, it hadn't changed very much from the 'belle époque' era when it was built and still provided a magical backdrop against which to portray these legendary cars.

Moss leads, in his works Maserati 250F, from the Lancia-Ferraris of Fangio and Castellotti, followed by the Vanwall of Harry Schell and Jean Béhra in another Maserati.

"The Maserati 250F was one of the nicest and easiest cars to drive. A far nicer car to drive than the Mercedes-Benz W196. Probably the most user-friendly Grand Prix car that I ever drove. That and the P25 BRM. It handled very well. At Monaco I chose to have a four speed box rather than five, because I could cut down on a couple of changes. I thought that was a better thing to do as it had a magnificent engine. Maximum speed at Monaco was only 130mph - nothing really. You could just get through the tunnel flat, which was quite exciting!" **Sir Stirling Moss**

Private Collection (32" x 20")

Collection: Mr. & Mrs. H. Bell (36" x 24")

AUTUMN RIDE OUT

I have quite a penchant for mixing horses and cars together in my pictures and often put them in this type of setting. Although my early efforts were of a more abstract nature, I still think of myself starting out as a landscape painter and it is very satisfying to portray the moods and seasons of the English countryside, as well as the sun-baked colours of Continental villages.

The car here is a Lagonda LG6 Rapide of about 1938 but the setting is intentionally timeless.

AN EVENING CHAT

I started painting these Casino Square night scenes when I was exhibiting every year at the Hôtel de Paris in Monaco in the 1990s. I try to conjure up that evocative, glamorous, hedonistic and, quite possibly, completely imaginary era when the sort of people who could afford to frequent Monte Carlo wouldn't dream of going to the Casino or out to dine without dressing correctly. And, of course, just as today, there is no better place to see the latest in exotic machinery.

Fortunately, my pleasure in painting these scenes has been matched by their acceptance by my patrons and clients and I have now painted Casino Square, with different cars and groups of people from just about every viewpoint there is.

CASINO SQUARE

Collection: Mr. J. Sives (40" x 24")

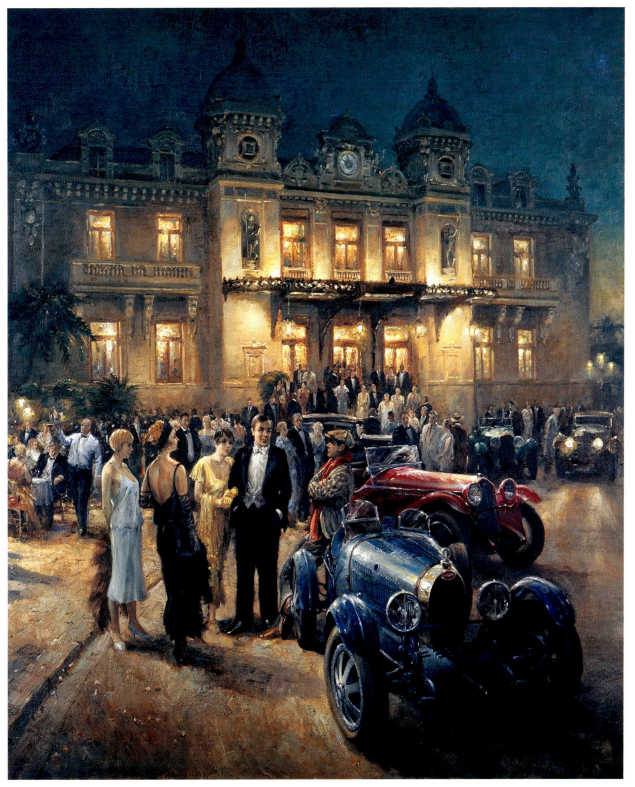

Collection: Mr. J. Sives (36" x 28")

PLACE DE L'OPERA

A lthough there is a car in this picture, a Delage in fact, it isn't really an automobile painting at all. It is a painting of the atmosphere of a wet, lamp-lit night, created almost entirely in sepia with just a hint of red in the lady's coat and blue/black in the Delage's wings, and, of course, everything disintegrating and disappearing in the sparkle and glare of the lights and reflections of the wet roads and pavements.

ARC DE TRIOMPHE

Collection: Mr. G. Waunford-Brown (16" x 12")

Collection: Mr. T. Fearn (16" x 12")

111

TARUFFI AT RAVENNA 1957

I have attempted to make this painting a scene of overall urgent action. Taruffi comes to a halt with a haze of blue smoke coming off the rear brakes, officials crouch down to stamp his road book, a photographer runs to picture him driving away and other officials raise hands and flags at the next car up. All of this combines to give tension and urgency to the picture.

As for the story behind the picture, that is well known. Taruffi, already 50-years-old, is taking part in his 14th Mille Miglia and has promised his wife that he will stop racing if he wins. Win he does, possibly with the help of team orders from Enzo Ferrari, and he keeps his promise but, due to the Marquis de Portago's terrible accident, it is to be the last ever Mille Miglia.

"Taruffi - very good sports car driver, one of the best and especially good in something like the Mille Miglia." **Sir Stirling Moss**

Private Collection (16" x 12")

LE MANS ORIGINAL

The inspiration to paint this picture came whilst looking through one of the Classic Car Profiles series published some years ago. I noticed in a photograph of the Frazer Nash parked in front of the pits at Le Mans that they had the garage next to the winning Ferrari. The idea of having both cars in the pits at the same time seemed too good to pass up.

The cars at this time were known as the Frazer Nash High Speed model and one was purchased by ex-racing motor cyclist, Norman Culpan, who entered the car for Le Mans in 1949. His co-driver was H. J. Aldington, owner of Frazer Nash Ltd, and with, therefore, works backing, the pair bought the car home in third place.

On the strength of this achievement, the name of the production cars was changed to Frazer Nash Le Mans Replica and a legendary model was born.

Collection of the Artist   *(16" x 12")*

Collection: Mr. A. Stephenson (16" x 12")

LOTUS ELAN

One of the things I particularly like about this painting is the contrast between the brightly coloured car and the lovely mellow old brick and stone of the entrance to Alan Stephenson's home. Something about the shape of the Elan leaves one in no doubt that it is made out of plastic or, at least, glass re-enforced plastic, emphasising, somehow, how ultra-typical it was of its period.

Having driven this particular car, I can certainly confirm the reputation they had at the time of being just about the quickest means of transport between two points it was then possible to buy.

"The Elan Sprint is another very special painting to me. I had an Elan in the early '70s when I met my wife, and when we married the Elan had to go. So now, having the car back, and having Alan's sensitive interpretation with the car on the drive at our home, encapsulates so many memories for me - it's invaluable!"
Alan Stephenson

INTERNATIONAL TROPHY '49

This is a picture of R. F. Wright in his Lagonda LG45 Rapide taking part in the Daily Express International Trophy meeting at Silverstone in 1949. It was commissioned by the new owner of the car just after he had bought it at auction. In the early years of motoring competitions after the Second World War, R. F. Wright campaigned this car quite extensively in both races and hillclimbs and in this major event, up against stiff works-entered opposition, he still managed to finish 12th. The race was won by Leslie Johnson in one of the latest Jaguar XK 120s but car number six in the picture, driven by Prince Bira, dropped out with tyre problems.

I have tried to heighten the period feel with the photographer's large, unwieldy camera and the 'milk churn' petrol cans on the pit counters.

Collection: Mr. W. Roberts (24" x 16")

GAIETY NIGHTS

This is the view looking from the Strand up Aldwych but the Gaiety Theatre, I am afraid, no longer stands there, having been replaced by a modern office block or bank. However, in the late thirties, it is easy to imagine the area to be a blaze of lights and bustle and elegance. That is the feeling I have attempted to convey. I could have called it Lagonda Nights with my old M45 on the right and a beautiful V12 Drophead on the left.

This painting featured in my 2005 London Exhibition and, as always, prior to the opening I sent out catalogues to my mailing list. Craig Davis rang immediately from America and bought the painting from the catalogue illustration. It transpired that only the week before he had bought a red V12 Drophead Lagonda. For once, perfect timing!

EVENING ON THE STRAND

Collection: Mr. P. Neumark (16" x 12")

Collection: Mr. C. Davis (30" x 24")

HECTIC MOMENTS

Here, I have tried to illustrate the frantic but stage-managed confusion of a night-time Ferrari pit stop. Gendebien looks at someone giving last-minute advice or information behind the car while the 'plombeurs' seal the petrol cap after the fuel stop. In front, a mechanic drags away a jack whilst on the right another looks up from hammering on a wheel nut. On the pit counter figures shout instructions, ask questions and the whole is lit in stark highlight and shadow to heighten the drama.

This is the Gendebien/Frère TR 3-litre which, in 1960, led Ferrari's total domination of the Le Mans 24-Hour race, having five out of the first seven cars home, the intruders being Clark and Salvadori in an Aston Martin.

Private Collection (34" x 20")

Collection: Mr. P. Read (36" x 24")

GOODWOOD NINE HOURS 1953

I have used long shadows and warm hues to indicate late evening in this picture of the Goodwood pits. Number four was the winning Aston Martin DB3S driven by Reg Parnell, seen here by the pit counter with co-driver Eric Thompson in the car, receiving instructions from John Wyer.

Meanwhile, Peter Collins pulls out in car number six, which he shared with Pat Griffith, on his way to second place. In the background, behind the Second World War aircraft hangers, the Sussex Downs are lit by the setting sun.

ASTON PIT STOP, GOODWOOD NINE HOURS

Collection: The Street Gallery (10"x 8")

HEADING FOR ARNAGE

This is the Ferrari GTO of Pierre Noblet and Jean Guichet at the right hander just after the pits at Le Mans in 1962 when they brought the car home in second place behind the 330TRI/LM of Phil Hill and Olivier Gendebien.

Darkness has eliminated all the superfluous background detail which is left as a suggestion through the light and the half-seen grandstand silhouette, allowing the car to be the only recognisable object in the painting and yet still it manages to avoid being just a portrait of a car.

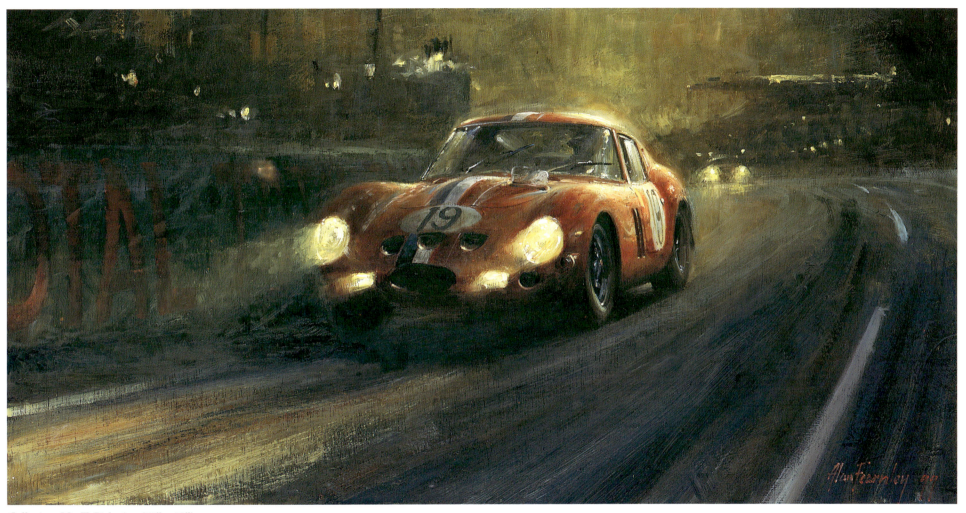

Collection: Mr. T. Pickering (20" x 10")

SUMMER SHOWER

A romantic little painting of a couple sheltering under a tree whilst he's taken care to keep the seats dry in his Riley. In this picture, I worked hard to capture the feeling of damp, limpid air and the sparkle that appears as the sun starts to break through after the rain.

Collection: Mr. K. H. Price (16" x 12")

Collection: Mr. A. Brownridge (16" x 12")

COFFEE BREAK

This picture is based on the most simple of ideas - a little Riley parked outside a pavement café. What could be more simple than that but, for various reasons, I think, it turned out as a most successful small painting. The ease of the figures in a mixture of light and shade, the shadow cast over the car and awning, odd details like the bald waiter and the man leaning on his bicycle all combined to create a picture that, for me, works really well.

ONE DAY MI AMORE

I imagine that most of us have done this in our youth - and quite possibly much more recently as well - that is to say, gazed longingly at someone else's exotic Ferrari. Though we did not, necessarily, have the girlfriend hanging round our neck whilst we did it.

When I was the age of the youngsters portrayed here my envious looks were cast at machines like Jaguar XK 120s. Now I own an XK 120, they are directed at things like GTOs, SWBs and 450Ss and unfortunately, I fear, envious looks are as near as I'm going to get.

Collection: Mr. M. Masters (30" x 20")

133

1914 MERCEDES

This is an early painting compared with most of those in this book, but it is one I have always liked. Visually, I enjoy the period, with men fighting machines on open roads and rough unmade surfaces.

The picture is based quite closely on a well-known photograph, which is something I never do nowadays. I have added the colour, of course, the second and third cars and the group with the bicycle to the right. The car is a 1914 Grand Prix Mercedes taking part in, and winning, the French Grand Prix of that year. It was driven by Christian Lautenshlager.

This was the last race before the First World War as four weeks later Archduke Ferdinand was assassinated and war was declared.

Private Collection (30" x 20")

EARLY HOURS

This is a rather different view of Casino Square at Monaco to the others in this book and, I must admit, it's a view that requires a considerable streak of imagination to be acceptable.

However, if one does accept the degree of artistic licence taken with the real Monte Carlo, then I think it is a very satisfying picture with the couple enjoying the last of their Champagne before driving off in their beautiful Zagato-bodied Alfa Romeo 8C Sports.

Private Collection (36" x 20")

Collection: Mr. J. Mason (30" x 18")

BRIEF ENCOUNTER

The commission for this painting was to devise a picture with a classic car that suggested the film 'Brief Encounter' and this was the interpretation that resulted.

The locomotive is, harking back to my days as Chairman of the *Guild of Railway Artists,* a Castle Class of the Great Western Railway. The car is a Mk V Jaguar and the man is lighting the cigarette for his girlfriend, as was obligatory in those pre-political correctness days.

ON THE GRID

This painting of Schumacher on the grid in his Ferrari is slightly out of context in this book but has a rather amusing story associated with it. It was exhibited at my one man show in Monaco in 1997. Before the exhibition, my then agent and publisher, the late-David Mills, decided to publish it as a limited edition print and the whole edition was printed, checked and signed by myself.

At the exhibition a young lady, who was helping with the office work, came over to me and said quietly, "I hope you don't mind me mentioning it Alan, but on that painting you've spelt Ferrari wrong". I dashed to it and, sure enough, there on the umbrella I'd got the Rs in the wrong order. I was horrified and, as we had already sold several prints, there was nothing else for it but to go to David and confess, to prepare him for an expected stream of complaints.

He thought for a minute and then came up with the perfect solution. "Don't worry," he said, "If anyone complains, I'll tell them you were drunk!"

As far as I'm aware, no-one else has ever noticed.

Private Collection (16" x 12")

HOLIDAY SNAPSHOT

Here are our friends, the Turners, with their XK 150 on the quayside at Villefranche, near Nice, where they have their holiday home. We met Ray and Judy as fellow members of the XK Club and, like many others, they became friends and then clients. When they first mentioned having their grandchildren in the picture, I was a little apprehensive. As a general rule, the younger a person is, the less defined and developed their features and consequently the more difficult it is to grasp a likeness in a portrait. However, I'm relieved to say, the end result was declared a success, helped by a background of the warm terracotta colours of the Côte d'Azur.

Collection: Mr. & Mrs. R. Turner (24" x 16")

Collection: Viscount Cowdray (40" x 28")

144

THE COWDRAY EQUIPE

L ord Cowdray approached me early in 2006 to see if I would take on the commission of painting him with his family and some of his cars.

I am not sure I knew just how many people were involved when I said yes, but, as can be seen here, it turned out to be seven, which was quite a daunting prospect. However, all turned out well after a little fine tuning on one of the faces and I think that the idea of the action in the figures, which I believe was Lord Cowdray's, worked very well with so complicated a scene.

Needless to say, as a setting, the Cowdray Park motor house with his two famous low-drag E-types, CUT 7 the Dick Protheroe prototype and 49 FXN the Lumsden/Sargent Lightweight, and a Ferrari California Spyder would be difficult to improve on.